EVERGLADES TIME'S DISCIPLINE

EVERGLADES | TIME'S DISCIPLINE

MARY PECK MERLIN PRESS

A Discipline

Turn toward the holocaust, it approaches
on every side, there is no other place
to turn. Dawning in your veins
is the light of the blast
that will print your shadow on stone
in a last antic of despair
to survive you in the dark.
Man has put his history to sleep
in the engine of doom. It flies
over his dreams in the night,
a blazing cocoon. O gaze into the fire
and be consumed with man's despair,
and be still, and wait. And then see
the world go on with the patient work
of seasons, embroidering birdsong
upon itself as for a wedding, and feel
your heart set out in the morning
like a young traveler, arguing the world
from the kiss of a pretty girl.
It is the time's discipline to think
of the death of all living, and yet live.

WENDELL BERRY

Before South Florida was developed, one continuous sheet of water covered the southern half of the Florida peninsula. That was long before the pavement was laid down, before the condominiums blocked sunrise on the Atlantic beaches, before the population exploded, and before that flow of water was violently and repeatedly altered by the visible work of the Army Corps of Engineers, and less visibly by the sugar industry. Less than half the original Everglades survived development, and that was declared a National Park in 1947, ten years before my family moved to Ft Lauderdale. The Everglades flowed over and through limestone buried under the street where I lived. Growing up in an air-conditioned world, I was absolutely divorced from the beauty, mystery, and sensuality that the Everglades— barely an hour away from my house—held. I only knew of the place by name, and the day after graduating from high school I left for the West. I was glad to go, but eventually, reluctantly, I returned to Florida, and on that visit when I was in my thirties made my first trip to the Everglades. This was my introduction to a nearly untamed piece of earth. It left me with a desire for more time to explore the place on foot, and for the stillness that resulted from simply being there. It was never quiet, but the traffic of alligators and birds, the industry of insects were intriguing and welcome. This was the beginning of an acquaintance with a realm at once rawer and gentler than the wholly human and mechanized world I had grown up in so nearby. In stark contrast to the attenuated and frenetic feel of life in Ft. Lauderdale, the fecundity of the Everglades corrected a great imbalance. More than an introduction to a once wild place, it was an exponential enlargement of the world as I had known it. Those days in the Everglades determined much of the course of my life because there the living world became so much more than human.

I returned to the Everglades several times over the next decade. I explored with people who had known the area intimately, and years before it became a National Park. By the 1920s many of the Everglades bird species, and the alligator, had been nearly hunted to extinction. The alligator and some bird species were in a period of recovery when I first saw the Everglades in 1984, but I saw nothing close to the spectacle, in number and variety, of birds that Audubon, and others following him, described seeing in the 1830s. I walked the old dikes that remain from one attempt to drain the Everglades, waded into the sloughs, and my sneakers sucked through the in-between land/water of dark, warm peat. I was immersed in a constant shifting stream of sights, sounds, and smells. Ethereal bromeliads that lived on air, thin cactus that spiraled twenty feet high, strangler figs that grew from an aerial root and, true to their name, strangled the host of that aerial root; poisonwood trees that dripped their blister-causing sap in the rain; at least forty-three kinds of mosquitoes, alligators, deer, flying squirrels, orchids, snakes, more than a hundred different bird species; pristine, wide beaches at Cape Sable, a jaw-dropping combination of birds, plants, insects, mammals. On the same day it was possible to move through swamp that felt eerily prehistoric and on to a calm bay, to the absolutely sublime.

Even in its diminished size and state, the Everglades were still forbidding, wild, and deeply satisfying. Now, more than thirty years after I went to the Everglades for the first time, it is further and seriously degraded. If I walked there today I would notice changes, and I would still see beauty and mystery— now mixed with the mystery and certainty of change.

MARY PECK, 2016

EVERGLADES: THE BEAUTIFUL REBUKE

William deBuys

Seen from the altitude of a satellite or from the abstract perspective of a mapmaker, the peninsula of South Florida presents the profile of an aging manatee. Lake Okeechobee is the clouded, lone eye. The limestone ridge supporting the core of Miami stretches down the coast like a thin spade of nasal bone. Where the peninsula yields to saltwater, the manatee's muzzle gives way to a beard of mangroves, and the keys dribble from its runny snout. The broad jowls, speckled as though by the roots of whiskers but in fact pocked by ponds and hammocks, represent the not-quite-land, not-quite-water of Marjorie Stoneman Douglas's legendary "River of Grass."

Like an actual manatee, south Florida is aquatic. And like a manatee, south Florida, within the time-frame of its geological existence, has spent more of its life underwater than at the surface. It moves slowly. It is fond of submergence, and the tea leaves of climate prediction tell us that South Florida, like a world-weary manatee, is now sinking beneath the waves again.

Three dominant "currents" shape the life of the peninsula. The first is—or was—one of the most singular and remarkable movements of freshwater to be found anywhere on the planet. It arose in central Florida, just south of where Orlando stands today, where a multitude of creeks and seeps merged into the Kissimmee River and flowed lazily, at times circuitously, southward, ultimately filling Lake Okeechobee. The lake,

for its part, possessed not so much an outlet as simply a rim, which it commonly—and sometimes spectacularly—overflowed to the south, discharging its waters onto an enormous, board-flat plain. There the spilling waters spread into a nearly uniform, sixty-mile-wide sheet, which grew waist-deep under the tumultuous thunderstorms of summer. The waters ran—or more accurately, crept—ever southward, trending slightly to the west, through scrubs of pond apple and other gnarled swamp brush but eventually into and through a saw grass prairie that spread from horizon to horizon. These endless grassy glades—*Everglades*—stretched a hundred and fifty miles, abutting cypress swamps and low pine ridges along its margins. The scale was spectacular. As more than a few early explorers dejectedly attested, a man might pick out some faint marker at the limit of sight, slog for a day or more to get there, and then, from the marker, looking forward, see only more of what he had just passed. His struggle earned him nothing, for nothing had changed. The same grass, the same water, the same horrific insects and implacable horizon still lay ahead. And then he might travel to another marker, and then another, and it was always the same. Soldiers and surveyors repeated this inchworm progress as many times as they could stand, yet the saw grass and the water (and the savvier native people) nearly always outlasted them.

That's how it used to be. And then came steam-powered and later diesel-powered dredges, which accomplished the conversion of wilderness into real estate. The story of the ditching, draining, and diversion of the waters of the Everglades is the creation story of modern South Florida. It is a myth in reverse, an account, not of how a natural Eden came to be, but of how it was destroyed. To borrow a phrase from Carl Hiaasen, one of the region's most popular contemporary writers, it is the saga of "Paradise Screwed."

The Edenic view of South Florida, admittedly, is a late-twentieth-century notion. It depends on viewing the peninsula in ecological terms while at the same time purging yourself of any bias against habitats for which you, as a biological entity, are so poorly prepared that they seem a suburb of hell. Eden and hell, joined at the hip; that's the Everglades. Once you stop slapping mosquitoes and worrying about snakes, once dreams of generating wealth from sugarcane, oranges, tourism, and real estate are fully banished from thought, once all that is left before you is the vast twining of land and water and the oddly adapted plants and the mad, anarchic society of the creatures, once your focus sharpens to a bright sharp edge to see what climate, geology, and nature's relentless, competitive selections have made, then you stand like the Magi before a miracle.

The marvel of the Everglades resides in the whole, not the parts, although the parts are plenty marvelous. The swamp is home to staggering numbers of plants and animals, especially birds, but its diversity is only one aspect of its integral character. The Everglades (usually treated as a singular noun) is to wetlands what Kilimanjaro is to lonely mountains, the Amazon to rivers, or the Grand Canyon to cracks in the Earth. All of these icons, the Everglades included, cause us to catch our breath and consider their size and brawn, but most impressive of all their qualities is their singularity. Nothing remotely matches them. There is only one of each, and only one Everglades. No other leagues-wide, limestone-floored, slow-seeping, freshwater river is remotely comparable because none exists. The Everglades is a giant ecosystem with no close relatives, an evolutionary one of a kind, a gigantic anomaly, the coelacanth of living communities.

Oddly, although the 'Glades have their share of mammals—deer, raccoons, panthers, and more—they are preeminently the domain of lizard kin, both cold- and warm-blooded. The cold-bloods, of course, include the alligator, which is to the 'Glades what the lion is to the Serengeti, and whose bellow is analog to the big cat's roar. Or at least the alligator used to be King of the Swamp—more on that soon. The warm-bloods are even more ubiquitous. They include a profusion of winged dinosaur descendants, clad in feathery raiment, that once crowded the Everglades' sky (more on that soon, too). In the everglades, jewel-like warblers, tanagers, and buntings hardly catch the eye, for a parade of big, gaudy, flamboyant strutters steals nearly every scene. These are the many species of herons, egrets, and ibises, and most improbable of all, the roseate spoonbill, who are the Beau Brummells of the avian world, creatures so beautiful that a brutal industry, the plume trade, arose from traffic in their extravagant feathers, and it arose, no surprise, in the Everglades. Ultimately the emergence of an ecological conscience among Americans extinguished the plume trade, and the Everglades were at the center of the evolution of this consciousness. Stronger than ever, our ecological conscience continues to evolve today, but whether it can yet save the beauty of its birthplace remains to be seen.

Beauty and the beasts: there you have the Everglades in a nutshell. Imagine evenings reddened by flights of spoonbills while knots of gators huff and slither in the ooze. Hold in your mind's eye vast swaths of saw grass, of cypress, and of mangrove carpeting the earth, each one punctuated by its own kind of exquisite detail, an orchid here, a tree snail there, the bands of color on the snail shell offering a palette that nothing from Delft or Limoges can match. Part of the beauty of this quite literally *extra-ordinary* place is the beauty of its creatures' adaptation, the delicate web of interdependencies that bind the parts to the singular whole. The more delicate the threads, however, the more easily they are ruptured. The Everglade kite (now better known as the snail kite) suffers from such vulnerability. It evolved to subsist almost entirely on a diet of apple snails, a kind of freshwater mollusk, but as human manipulations have altered the hydrology of the Everglades, the supply of apple snails has declined, and so the kites have, too. And many of the kite's brethren in the creature world of the Everglades can lament a similar fate.

Diminished and comparatively desiccated, the Everglades persists as a kind of inundated Kansas of water, grass, and muck, where enough of the old vigor remains to suggest how things used to be, but not enough to assure that much of the old will last far into the future. With unusual candor, the brief guide distributed at the entrances to Everglades National Park states, "The Everglades is presently on life support, alive but diminished." Even diminished, the 'Glades are a Noah's ark of wetland wildlife and an ecological marvel. Nearly two hundred fifty miles south of the Kissimmee headwaters, they finally yield to a labyrinth of mangroves, edging the sea. The Everglades doesn't give out until the continent does. The mangrove jungle is their coda. It mediates the final transition from fresh to saltwater and from the underlying plateau of saturated limestone, where the freshwater flowed, to the shallows of Florida Bay.

This transition brings to the fore the second "current," which is really not a current but a sort of hydraulic wrestling match. The waters of the Everglades push down as they flow. They penetrate the pores of the limestone on which the peninsula is built, filling a great aquifer, and having filled it, they press outward. The vast reserves of freshwater that are housed in the limestone make possible the megalopolis of Miami, Fort Lauderdale, and West Palm Beach, the eighth largest conurbation in the United States. The nearly six million people who live amid that sprawl, as well as the millions of tourists who visit it each year, drink from the aquifer and from the surface waters that otherwise would recharge it. Nearly everyone on the west coast of the peninsula and in other nearby pockets of population does the same.

Here's where the plot thickens: the more the people of the peninsula drink and wash and flush, and the more they continue to divert the waters of the Everglades into their plumbing or out to sea, the less freshwater the aquifer holds. This is obvious. Less evident is the diminution of the hydraulic "head"—the gravity force of water bearing down—that pressurizes the aquifer. The weakened head means there is less outward "push" of south Florida's subterranean freshwater to counter the inward push of the saltwater that surrounds the peninsula on three sides. The result of this unequal shoving match is the steady intrusion of saltwater where freshwater used to be, which translates to the failure of wells and the increasing difficulty of opening new ones. It guarantees continuous water shortage for human populations, as well as a host of salt-driven ecological changes.

And then comes the problem of the third "current," which is minute and gradual, and utterly trumps the others. It is the upward rising of the sea, driven principally by climate change.

The matter is complicated and ramifies in multiple ways. A rising ocean helps the sea shove harder against the inland freshwater that Floridians, through both drainage and consumption, are so rapidly removing. In time the rising sea will overwhelm the outdated gates, locks, and other structures on canals and rivers that are intended to hold back a "head" of freshwater to counter saltwater intrusion. The scramble to elevate such structures to keep pace with the ocean's escalation will never end. And in a kind of domino effect, the rising sea will ever more aggressively erode the beaches that underpin the tourist industry, which in turn undergirds the economy, which provides the tax base, which funds the infrastructure, which keeps the drains and wells working, the highways diked, and the environment at bay. One day the dominoes will fall, perhaps blown down by a hurricane, perhaps tipped over by economic collapse, quite possibly succumbing to a combination of the two.

South Florida's options are limited. Unlike other regions where sea walls are effective, south Florida's limestone basement is as porous as a sponge. A rising ocean will transmit its pressure through the limestone beneath the foundation of the deepest barrier, pushing up the water table behind it to drown the backyards, and then the living rooms, of subdivisions far inland.

More blatantly, there is the issue of direct submergence.

The Army Corps of Engineers, abetted by the South Florida Water Management District, a state agency, carried out the draining of the Everglades. Today, in a reversal suggesting that the universe loves irony more than justice, the Corps is charged with the multi-billion-dollar "restoration" of what it has so far destroyed. As a result, the Corps is compelled to think about climate change. Officially, the agency projects a two-foot rise in sea level by 2100 as its "intermediate" scenario. At this level, most of Everglades National Park, all of the Ten Thousand Islands, and a large chunk of Big Cypress National Preserve would be inundated. They would simply vanish. A decent storm surge, meanwhile, would roll over nearly all developed property from Miami Beach southward. These eventualities will solve much of the restoration problem by rendering it moot, but only after the Corps has spent billions more.

Trouble is, as the National Research Council, a unit of the National Academies of Science and Engineering, points out in its review of restoration efforts in the Everglades, "The stability of the Greenland and Antarctic ice sheets has been a major element of uncertainty, and recent research in West Antarctica has reported more rapid rates of glacial melting than previously anticipated." This means the Corps' intermediate estimate of sea-level rise is almost certainly low.

By comparison, the "intermediate-high" projection by the National Oceanic and Atmospheric Administration (NOAA) takes into account some of the instability in the planet's great ice sheets and forecasts a rise in sea level of 3.9 feet by century's end. Were this to occur, virtually all of Everglades National Park, Big Cypress National Preserve, the Florida Keys, and several hundred miles of coastal development will exist only in memory. Much of the Tamiami Trail, the highway linking Miami to Florida's west coast, will have drowned, and a big new lake will glitter on the western, inland side of Miami, giving the city a foretaste of the island it is destined to become.

But wait. That's not all. The "highest sea level change scenario" forecast by NOAA, which the agency says "should be considered in situations where there is little tolerance for risk," entails a 6.6 foot rise and "reflects ocean warming and the maximum plausible contribution of ice sheet loss and glacial melting." Under this scenario, by 2100 the remains of Miami will be ringed by water, Hialeah will belong to the crocodiles, and, as was said of Luca Brasi in *The Godfather*, almost everything else in Florida south of Naples and Ft. Lauderdale will "sleep with the fishes."

The fact is, south Florida is going under. Only the timing remains in dispute.

A sense of inferiority nagged at citizens of the early American republic. Sure, they had political and economic freedoms that were the envy of many throughout the world, but the Old World had culture, and America didn't. The Old World had the ruins of Greece and Rome, cathedrals that were centuries old, ancient literatures, and a depth of history beside which the new American experience seemed unformed and immature. Americans might see themselves as a nation of the future, but when they compared their continent to Europe and thought about the hoary traditions they'd left behind, they half agreed with those who condescendingly called them "colonials."

The ideas that emerged as antidotes to this self-doubt had multiple roots. Romanticism and its philosophical offspring, Transcendentalism, contributed much, and so did the physical substance of the American continent. A distinguishing feature of Romanticism, the bundle of attitudes that swept western civilization in the nineteenth century, was its love for the sublime. The Classical period, which Romanticism supplanted, valued order, structure, and strict protocols. Its style of thinking followed lines as straight as the *allées* at Versailles. Romanticism, by contrast, hungered for the thrill of surprise and naked force. It craved the jolt of adrenaline, the *frisson* of fear, to be felt in the experience of crashing waves or a great storm. Some said the hand of the Divine was most evident in the violence of nature, and that wildness could therefore be a spiritual text. Some just wanted the intensity of being at the edge of control, of experiencing the full, creative, electric thrust of life. The feeling was sublimity itself.

Niagara Falls could deliver the feeling. So could the gloomy forests of the Adirondacks and the wild splendor of the Hudson River Valley, which soon gave its name to an American school of painting notable for its depiction of the sublime. Gradually, in the early days of the republic, America began to see itself as "Nature's nation." This emergent identity did not fully blossom until Americans had completed their continental migration and beheld the wonders of the Rockies and the Sierra Nevada. In those majestic places they found something to boast about that no European could claim. Who needed the marble columns of ancient Greece, when he could glory in the majesty of Yellowstone and Yosemite? Surely these were as sublime as any landscapes on Earth.

Proud of the continent they had conquered, Americans undertook to protect some of its more spectacular features. The effort began falteringly, but grew into a national movement. Yellowstone became a National Park in 1872. Yosemite was a state park for more than two decades before it became a national park in 1890. Other parks (and after 1891, forest reserves) added more jewels to the national crown, all of them majestic, inspiring, and sublime. The Grand Canyon, however, posed a problem. It possessed great sublimity, but it had it the wrong way—as a void, a hole in the earth—not as a presence, like a mountain. It did not become a national park until 1919, but the campaign for it (and the campaigns for other unusual places) helped stretch the meaning of what a park might be.

As these events were occurring, the word *ecology* crept slowly into the language, and the concepts underlying what we now call *biodiversity* began to take form. Romanticism didn't go away, but it gradually metamorphosed—some would say, sobered—into a modernism heavily influenced by science. Gradually, people began to accept the idea that the potential of a place to support rational, critical learning might have the same intellectual heft as ideas about inspiration and sublimity. Not far behind was the notion that the very fact of a thing's uniqueness, especially the uniqueness of a large, complex system, should earn it a particular kind of respect and thereby assure its right to exist.

When President Harry Truman dedicated a portion of the Everglades as the nation's twenty-seventh national park in 1947, he broadened the meaning of the national park system more or less to what it is today. As today's rangers will proudly tell you, the Everglades was the country's first "scientific" park. The long campaign for its protection touted the singularity of the freshwater ecosystem, perhaps the largest and most complex in the world. The ultimate anthem of the campaign— and the continuing refrain of efforts to add to the park and protect its systems—was Marjorie Stoneman Douglas's lyrical *The Everglades: River of Grass*, which begins,

There are no other Everglades in the world.

They are, they always have been, one of the unique regions of the earth, remote, never wholly known. Nothing anywhere else is like them: their vast glittering openness, wider than the enormous visible round of the horizon, the racing free saltness and sweetness of the massive winds, under the dazzling blue heights of space.

If Americans started over with our national parks, if we set about *now*, in the second decade of the twenty-first century, to organize a national system of extraordinary places from scratch, and if we were to do it based on current ecological understanding, where would we start? The Everglades would certainly come in at the top of our list. Or at least the Everglades *in its original condition* would earn one of the highest placements, maybe the highest. That part is easy. The harder task would be to rank the Everglades in its present degraded—and declining—state. With the system's current prospects so profoundly compromised, their most ardent advocates have to admit that the Everglades are a weak bet for survival. Even absent the specter of rising seas, the woes besetting the River of Grass are myriad.

For starters, the legendary populations of wading birds are only a tenth of what they used to be. The skies formerly darkened by clouds of herons, egrets, ibis, flamingos, spoonbills, and wood storks are now mostly clear. The species are still there (although don't hold your breath if you are waiting to see a flamingo), but the aerial regiments that once blotted out the sun have been whittled down to platoons on lonely patrol. Partly, they've been starved of fish, as the marshes and swamps have been starved of water. Partly, they suffer from loss of rookeries that have been sacrificed to coastal development. And probably large numbers of their young now fall prey to a predator their ancestors never had to watch out for.

That predator is the Burmese python (*Python bivittatus*), a snake native to forests and wetlands from eastern India to China, Vietnam, and Indonesia. Its home range is vast, but its population is declining broadly, and it is considered "critically endangered" in some of its native regions. Unfortunately, this is not the case in South Florida, where, once upon an undefined time, some idiot pet store owner or amateur "snake fancier" grew tired of coming up with a rabbit a day for his charming, cold-blooded "pets," which were on track to grow longer than a pickup truck. This Yahweh of reptiles released a pythonic Adam and Eve into the herpetological Eden of the Everglades. The snakes did more than prosper; they multiplied "like rabbits," with the effect that today there are no more rabbits in the Everglades—the swamp's population of lagomorphs has declined one hundred percent. Other small mammals—raccoons, bobcats, opossums—have declined as badly as the wading birds, down ninety percent or more, and the python appears to be a major cause. Deer, too, are now scarce, and a fawn is not a particularly big meal for a snake that can cross a country lane without its head and the tip of its tail being on the roadway at the same time. In one famously documented case, a thirteen-foot python managed to choke down a six-foot alligator. The snake's gluttony was ill-advised, however, as its stomach subsequently exploded in what one wag called "a gastronomical Vesuvius." Either that, or the gator was insufficiently dead when the python swallowed it and managed to claw at the snake's stomach from the inside, causing it to rupture, or . . . well, you be the judge: the postmortem photographs are easy to find on the Internet.

The Burmese python, now that it has replaced the alligator at the top of the Everglades food chain, may be the most influential exotic species in the Everglades, but it is by no means the only one to disturb the swamp's native ecological balances. The warm, subtropical climate and soupy, fecund environment have thrown out a welcome to dozens of plants and animals that the human chuckleheads at its margins have discarded, allowed to escape, or intentionally introduced. Melaleuca (also known as Australian paperbark), Brazilian pepper, Australian pine, and Old World climbing fern cumulatively infest hundreds of thousands of Everglades acres, and in these areas they have shifted the fire ecology to favor frequent, hot burns that reinforce their dominance at the expense of native plants. Animals as large as the Nile monitor, a lizard that can exceed five feet in length, and as small as the Mexican bromeliad weevil are similarly wreaking havoc on native biota, shifting relationships, like any self-respecting Darwinian agent, to advance their own perpetuation. It bears noting, however, that the agent of Everglades destruction need not be exotic. The more a system is hammered from the outside, the more vulnerable it becomes to perturbations of all kinds. An example: cattail reeds, which are native to North America but previously absent from the Everglades, have taken over immense areas thanks to phosphate pollution from both municipal waste and sugarcane production in the northern (which is to say, upstream) portion of the system. The unwanted nutrients are like steroids for the cattails, which then outgrow the plants (and thereby destroy the habitat of the animals) that were there before them.

Meanwhile, rising seas are not just a problem of the future; they are already transforming the Everglades' lowest elevations, causing mangrove forests to retreat from the coast and shift inland. One of the most closely watched arenas for sea-level rise is Cape Sable, where the shoreline has markedly eroded and freshwater marshes have grown brackish.

At least some South Florida communities are aware of the threat of rising seas. In October 2014, the city commission of South Miami voted to secede from the rest of Florida, forming a new state comprising twenty-four low-lying counties in the south of the state. The commission's main grievance is the unwillingness of the state government, based in Tallahassee, to address the threat of rising seas—or even admit the existence of climate change. Of course, the vote was a pretty much a grandstanding gesture with little significance beyond the next day's headlines, but for a fleeting moment, South Miami made its point.

And part of that point is that the political ecology of Florida may be harder to fix than anything in its biological portfolio. The same may be said for the political ecology of the United States as a whole. Neither Congress nor the state legislature has shown much capacity for addressing complex problems, least of all climate change. Interestingly, the Everglades is deeply, even centrally, entwined in the evolution of our current culture of uncompromising politics.

Readers will remember that Al Gore "lost" Florida in 2000 by a margin of only 537 votes, and as a result, George W. Bush, in one of the profoundest tipping points in recent American history, "won" the presidency thanks to a Supreme Court decision so peculiar that its authors said it should never be used as precedent for any other case.

One of the constituencies Gore failed to carry as he had hoped included environmentalists. Many deserted him because he did not condemn the efforts then in motion to develop a new international airport within the Everglades ecosystem near Homestead, Florida. Gore only promised "a balanced decision" when all the facts were in. Outraged, a large number of Everglades advocates voted for third-party candidate Ralph Nader, probably by the thousands and certainly in numbers larger than Bush's narrow and unverified margin of victory. Had the Everglades issue played differently, Gore would likely have become president. As it turned out, the Clinton administration, in its last days, killed the airport project that had killed the Gore campaign. The early years of the presidency of George W. Bush, meanwhile, saw the United States renounce the Kyoto Protocol on climate change, initiate the longest war in American history in Iraq, and take many forks down many roads far different from those it would have followed under a President Gore.

In December 2000, on the last day of arguments before the Supreme Court in Bush v. Gore, a momentous signing ceremony took place in the White House. For obvious reasons, Gore was otherwise occupied, but for eight years he had been a principal advocate for the most salient feature of the legislative act being celebrated. The bill, which included a potpourri of federal actions related to water, contained the Comprehensive Everglades Restoration Plan (CERP), the intended capstone to current efforts to reverse the decline of the South Florida environment. It represented the broadest, most complex, and—at $13.5 billion—the most expensive attempt at ecological restoration in human history.

Flash forward to 2014. According to the National Research Council, which is charged with evaluating the program's progress every two years, CERP has spent $4.25 billion from both federal and state sources but has made only "modest restoration progress focused along the edges of the

Everglades," while the core of the Everglades continue to suffer "ongoing degradation," each increment of which "could take many decades or longer to recover." Every delay, said the NRC, has been environmentally costly, yet obstacles to project implementation continue to mount. They include "increasingly frustrating financial, procedural, and policy constraints," by which is meant the failure of Congress and the Florida legislature to appropriate the funding they had previously promised, as well as multiple varieties of bureaucratic sloth and red tape, and successful lobbying by the enemies of the Everglades, notably the Florida real estate and sugar industries, to stall, hamstring, or otherwise derail needed restoration work.

In contrast to the slowness of the progress being made, said the NRC, the challenges posed by rising seas and invasive species, like the Burmese python, made rapid, immediate response imperative. It issued a clarion call for action, and the call rang out, but, after a while, newspaper headlines and TV reports shifted to other subjects, and the ringing stopped.

A century ago, the Everglades were seen as a kind of rebuke to Florida and even to the whole nation in that they steadfastly resisted the Herculean efforts that were devoted to draining and taming them. They refused to become "useful" to society. Now, in the second decade of the twenty-first century, the Everglades remains a rebuke as the great swamp resists being healed. All the king's horses and all the king's men have failed and continue to fail to put the shattered Humpty Dumpty ecosystem together again. The 'Glades are too big, too complex, too dynamic, and too far gone. The king, in this instance, has been shown to be a hollow power and the people of his kingdom to be a lumbering, selfish, and hubristic tribe. Things weren't supposed to work out this way, but they have.

In the Everglades the sky likes to stand on its head. Many are the days that wind-torn, ground-dragging, gunmetal clouds scrape across the wet plains. Anywhere else, you would expect to see such clouds high in the sky, but here the ether is strangely inverted: the stark clouds are low, and an immense sky shines above them blue and clear.

One day, under such a sky, I went for a paddle.

I slid my kayak into tea-dark water in a narrow gap among mangroves, climbed in, and shoved off. I was headed into Noah's world, where the Flood has never finished.

The mangrove is one of Earth's most enterprising organisms, for it is adept in stealing territory from the sea. In shallow salt and brackish water it stands on clusters of thumb-thick roots, from which it strides forward on still more roots, when conditions allow, to colonize the next inch or yard of sea-edge. Slowly it traps within its myriad stems all manner of storm- and tide-tossed sediment, shells, leaf litter, and debris to build up a spongy semblance of land. Of course, this only works if the sea stays roughly level. If the sea is rising, as it is in the Everglades, the mangroves lose their advantage and are forced to retreat.

From the air a mangrove swamp can look like a slice of brain: pathways twining, snaking, doubling back through dense, shapeless masses. It can have a positive-negative duplicity, retaining its pattern no matter if the water reverses to mangrove and the mangrove to water. To be lost in mangrove forest is to be thoroughly lost. No path leads for long in the direction it begins. Dead ends and turn backs are infinite. Your path to safety may begin in a direction opposite the one your compass urges you to go. And no matter where you turn, everything looks the same as everything else. A wall of slender stems and slenderer shadows surrounds you. The wall is interlaced and impenetrable, with a top too tall to see over, and a bottom that is no bottom at all, just a leg-breaking, foot-piercing tangle of roots, mud, and water, bountifully endowed with unseen insects and reptiles.

I follow a water trail through the mangroves marked by white plastic pipes driven into the muck at major turns, or at least at most of them. There are hundreds of turns and hundreds of markers. I grow fond of the sight of white plastic. The trick is not to lose track of the last one before the next comes in view. Often I turn about—not an easy maneuver where the mangroves close in—and return to a previous marker in order to search, by a different route, for its successor. Sometimes the mangroves on either side merge overhead, and I glide down tight, sun-dappled tunnels, keeping a wary eye out for snakes overhead.

For long stretches, I uncouple my kayak paddle at its middle joint, and use half of it to blade along as though in a canoe. There isn't room enough to manage the paddle at full length. Each narrows eventually debouches into a pond or small lake, and for a time I am able to scull forward with power on both sides, all the while searching for the next white pipe, the next assurance that I have not strayed from the one and only path that will take me where I intend, and that also, in a day's time, will take me home.

Another tunnel. Another pond. Another marker.

A small snake floats just inside the entrance to the next tunnel. Snakes float well. If you had a single lung, like a snake's, which extended inside your body for a third of your length, you would float well, too. I glide slowly forward. The snake does not give way. It is perhaps two feet long, and the red and black geometry of the pattern on its back recalls a Hopi pot. It shows no fear, no concern whatever. Entering the tunnel, I glide within inches of it, and as I slide past, I see its beady eyes and the darkened tip of its tail. I especially note the broad triangular head, which I realize must be the head of a viper, a rattlesnake probably. I do not pause or linger. When I come to the next opening in the mangroves, I rue that I did not stop to observe the snake and take its photograph—to watch it as a proper naturalist would. But my sorrow is shallow. I also reason that a snake swimming so far from actual land must be adept at climbing mangroves, and that a mangrove-climbing snake might just as easily climb into my boat, not that a snake would aggress in such a way, but that, given the confusion that arises when snakes and humans mutually scare each other in close quarters . . . well, it feels good to be out in the open, with the unmolested snake behind me. Four poisonous snakes inhabit the Everglades: the rare and reclusive coral snake, the water moccasin or cottonmouth, with which I am familiar, the eastern diamondback rattlesnake, whose cousin, the western diamondback, I also know well, and the pygmy rattler, whose acquaintance, I realize, I have just made.

I briefly consider doubling back for another look, but suddenly the sky fills with birds, small birds, swirling infinite clouds of them. They are tree swallows, swarming thick enough to blot out the blue heavens. There must be at least ten thousand of them. Or twenty thousand. They are uncountable. They billow up and down, left and right. Billow after billow intersecting other billows, the birds wheeling as one, dividing, merging, and then dividing again. Their dance continues to the limit of sight, and no doubt continues beyond. I have seen many a dense flight of birds but never anything so profuse as this. When Audubon visited Cape Sable in 1832, the sky filled at least as impressively with herons, egrets, ibises, spoonbills, and storks, a sight no longer to be seen. The great painter-naturalist wrote, "The flocks of birds that covered the shelly beaches, and those hovering overhead, so astonished us that we could for a while scarcely believe our eyes." And when he saw a hot-pink cloud of flamingos: "Reader, could you but know the emotion than then agitated my breast. I thought I had now reached the height of my experience."

Ah well, I say to myself, thinking of Audubon, tree swallows are not wading birds, but they are spectacular in their way.

The water trail leads out through progressively larger ponds until I am on the edge of a winding, continuous lake of open water that my map says stretches westward scores of miles to the Gulf of Mexico. Somewhere far to the north of me (and upstream) lies the "ridge and slough" zone, where pine and hardwood hammocks rise like islands from the river of grass and where alligators, basking in their wallows, look from a distance like scraps of blown truck tire. In all directions I see only mangroves and water, and, pausing in the lee of a thicket, I feel the Big Silence of the Everglades beginning to descend. I am in the heart of the largest wilderness area east of the Mississippi and the nation's third largest national park.

After a short rest, I return to open water and turn bow-first into a splashy headwind. Another twisting mile and a hundred white-pipe markers go by, and around yet another bend, I spy, across the lake, the straight lines and right-angled shape of a chickee, a small, roofed deck, raised above the water (and named for the raised-platform dwellings of the region's Seminoles and Miccosukees). The chickee will be my home for the night.

Unfortunately, soon after I unload at the chickee, the Big Silence takes a hit. Off to the northeast, a couple of small, prop-driven planes practice dives and climbs, perhaps in a sham dogfight, as noisy as a real one. Their racket sounds like the soundtrack to the movie *Midway*, minus machine guns and bombs, and it gives the impression that the swamp is under attack, which of course, in a different way, it is. I brew a cup of tea and putter with my gear, finding it strange to hang a bladder of water from a rafter of the chickee, the same as I would hang a bag of food in bear country. The reason for this precaution is a good one. The chickee stands only a dozen yards from a wall of mangroves that the map asserts is the edge of a massive forest. I have been told that in this brackish world raccoons and wood rats are perpetually starved for freshwater and will risk gators, drowning, and angry humans to get it.

The airplanes' din continues for an hour or more, but as the sun sinks, the swamp's silence—and enchantment—returns. Scattered grebes paddle the lake, diving with comic suddenness and, minutes later, unpredictably popping back to the surface far from where they began. A lone coot guards the entrance of a distant cove. Then something breaks the water not twenty yards away. I turn in time to see nostrils sink from sight, as ripples radiate outward. A large dark shape dissolves below them. A manatee? I hope so. The big, placid sea mammals are as extravagantly odd as a pangolin or a bird of paradise. A manatee in these waters would be a robust sign of ecological intactness.

A mullet jumps by the mangrove edge, and the splash sounds large.

I look at the wall of mangrove stems and leaves. The uniformity of its complexity—if those contradictory ideas can be linked—seems to invite a kind of meditation. It is not easy to *see* into a mass that is so densely packed. Mangroves, jungles, and close-packed forests present a special problem for our savannah-evolved sense of sight. We see walls where other creatures see endless depths—space in three dimensions. Our eyes hunger for a focal center, a point around which to organize the visual data we perceive. But rarely (as the photographs of Mary Peck show us) do the mangroves, cypress swamps, or jungled hammocks of the Everglades offer such comfort. Instead, we have to learn (again, as Peck shows) to look at them afresh, teasing out their proliferous architecture, and gazing deeper, and still deeper, through the illusory surface of the wall.

I hear a muted sigh, a long gasping exhalation. Slowly I turn. A large turtle (a Florida softshell, by the crook of its nose) hangs in the water by the chickee, its snorkel nostrils and periscope eyes barely breaking the surface. No doubt this is the "manatee" of a half hour ago. The turtle watches me, and through the mirrored surface of the stained water I can see the outline of its carapace, easily two feet from stem to stern. An instant later, and without evident movement of limb or tail, it noiselessly sinks from sight.

Once long ago, I awoke at dawn on a jet plane descending to refuel at Manaus, in the heart of Amazonia. I watched through the window as we negotiated a thousand feet of clouds. When we broke below them, the confluence of the Amazon and Rio Negro burst into view. I saw a chaos of water and not-quite-land, another slice of Earth-brain, its emerald vegetation in riot. The Sundarbans of Bangladesh and India, delta country where the waters of the Brahmaputra, Padma, and Meghna Rivers merge, are an equally great wetland region, which one day I hope to see, but here, alone on my chickee, deep in the Everglades, I have no longing to be elsewhere and, yes, I feel a pulse of national pride to be where I am. In this moment, I would not trade this chickee for the Acropolis. Far away, I see an osprey hovering high above some cousin bay to this one. A lone cormorant, wings beating metronomically, sallies into a sunset that burns the horizon white.

Suddenly, as though in chorus, catbirds cry out from the mangroves, five or six within a stone's throw. Their call is more a bleat than a song. A minute later, still in unison and just as suddenly, they stop. Farther off, I hear the mewing of more of them, and beyond those, still more, as their outcry rolls through the mangroves in a vocal wave. The spectacular briefness of the birds' clamor leaves a mysterious void in the silence.

Now the sun's light is gone, and a thousand shades of darkness lie upon the water. From within the mangroves come more and bigger splashes, which I cannot explain. A cricket-like chirr rises to consciousness. Can crickets survive even here? A few mosquitoes hover and whine, but a gentle breeze and my head net keep them at bay.

Planets and stars appear: Cassiopeia, the Pleiades, soon Orion. A stir of water and another sigh of exhalation: the turtle is back. A shooting star strobes the firmament. Then a satellite hurries across the constellations. On the far southern horizon, I can see the arc of lights marking the Keys and the illuminated stripe of the highway that joins them.

Dashes of starlight play upon the rippled lake, as full darkness descends. The Big Silence now embraces the stars, as the doomed beauty of the Everglades, one of the marvels of the world, yields to onrushing night.

SOURCES

Marjorie Stoneman Douglas, *The Everglades: River of Grass*, Pineapple Press (60th Anniversary Edition), 1947, 2007.

Michael Grunwald, *The Swamp: The Everglades, Florida, and the Politics of Paradise*, Simon and Schuster, 2006.

Carl Hiaasen, *Dance of the Reptiles*, Vintage Books, 2014.

R. Moss, J. Obeysekera, A. Sallenger, and J. Weiss. 2012. *Global Sea Level Rise Scenarios for the US National Climate Assessment*. NOAA Tech Memo OAR CPO-1. 37 pp.

National Research Council, *Progress Toward Restoring the Everglades*: *The Fifth Biennial Review*. National Academies Press, 2014. Downloadable at http://www.nap.edu. A. Parris, P. Bromirski, V. Burkett, D. Cayan, M. Culver, J. Hall, R. Horton, K. Knuuti.

Surging Seas: Sea Level Rise Analysis by Climate Central, *Submergence Risk Map*, access at http://ss2.climatecentral.org.

Merlin Press LLC

ISBN 978-0-692-69106-9

Front flap: Map of the State of Florida, 1856. HistoryMiami Museum; Steel engraving, prepared by order of the Honorable Jefferson Davis, Secretary of War. The museum's copy was the gift of Marjory Stoneman Douglas.

The photographs were made in Big Cypress National Preserve and Everglades National Park between 1984 and 1994 using a Fujica Panorama G617 camera with 120 film which produces four 6cm × 17cm images per roll. The images in this book were scanned from silver gelatin prints made by the photographer.

The book was designed by Catherine Mills Design, Seattle, and the typefaces are Dispatch Extended and Filosofia. The duotone negatives were made by Thomas Palmer, Newport, Rhode Island. The books were printed by Meridian Printing, East Greenwich, Rhode Island, under the supervision of Danny Frank. The manuscript editor was Elizabeth Hadas.